PRIMER

MICHAEL AARON PIANO COURSE

LESSONS

◆

Especially designed for the early-age beginner

◆

FOREWORD

THE MICHAEL AARON PIANO PRIMER was written especially for young children. Many years of specialization in the teaching of children have made the author keenly aware of three essentials in a teacher's approach. They are UNDERSTANDING, SYMPATHY and ENCOURAGEMENT. These thoughts have guided and influenced the author in his general plan and selection of material for this book.

Features

1. Storybook introduction to the first rudiments of music.
2. Development of rhythm through the clapping and counting of "Rhythm Patterns."
3. Smooth step-by-step progression from MIDDLE C illustrated by the use of many clear and simple charts.
4. Music which appeals to children.

CONTENTS

Introduction to Music

Note

– I am a music note.

Staff

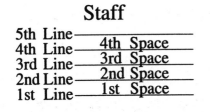

5th Line
4th Line — 4th Space
3rd Line — 3rd Space
2nd Line — 2nd Space
1st Line — 1st Space

– I live on a staff made of five lines and four spaces.

Line Note

– If my home is on a line, I am called a LINE NOTE.

Space Note

– If my home is on a space, I am called a SPACE NOTE.

Treble Clef

When you see the TREBLE CLEF sign (𝄞) in this book, you play the notes with the RIGHT HAND. Another name for the treble clef is G clef.

Bass Clef

When you see the BASS CLEF sign (𝄢) in this book, you play the notes with the LEFT HAND. Another name for the bass clef is F clef.

Grand Staff

The treble and bass staffs are joined together by a BRACE to form the GRAND STAFF.

Measures

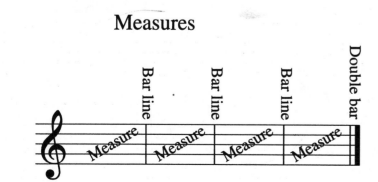

Music is divided into MEASURES. Each measure is separated by a BAR LINE. A DOUBLE BAR LINE shows the end of a piece.

Musical Alphabet

The musical alphabet consists of seven letters, A B C D E F G. These letters are used over and over.

Notice that the C is always at the left of the two black keys. The C closest to the middle of the piano is called MIDDLE C.

Sometimes MIDDLE C
is played with the RIGHT HAND.

Sometimes MIDDLE C is
played with the LEFT HAND.

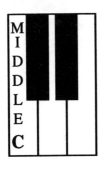

MIDDLE C for
right hand.

MIDDLE C for
left hand.

Time Signature

The numbers at the beginning of a piece of music are called a TIME SIGNATURE.

Top number – number of beats per measure.
Bottom number – kind of note that receives 1 count.

♩ – I am called a quarter note.

𝄽 – I am called a quarter rest. A rest is a sign for silence.

2/4 – There are 2 counts in each measure.

– A quarter note (♩) gets ONE count.

– A quarter rest (𝄽) also gets ONE count.

The Bass Drum

Count 1   2   1   2   1   2   1   2

Clap hands for each note. Do NOT clap the rests.

Now say the words and clap hands for each note.

Left   Left   Left Right Left

HAND POSITION

Place your fingers over the keys as shown in the drawing below and you will be in the correct position to play "March of the Middle C Twins." Notice that both thumbs are placed on Middle C.

FINGERING

In piano music a number may be placed near a note to show you which finger to use.

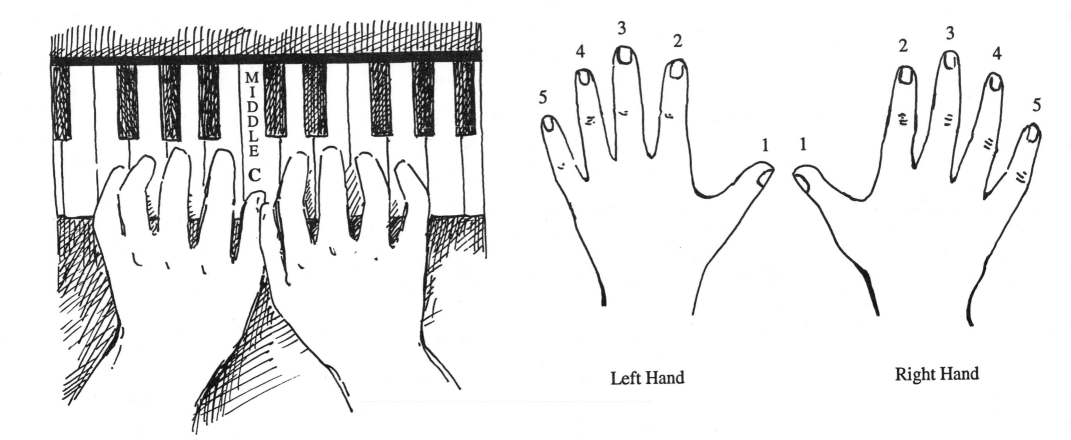

Left Hand   Right Hand

March of the Middle C Twins

New Notes – B and D

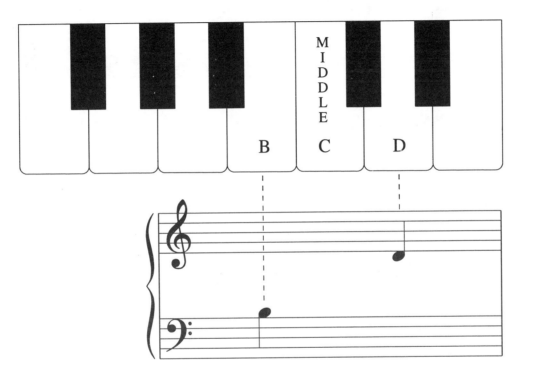

My name is B. I am just BELOW C, to the right of the THREE BLACK NOTES. My note is in the space ABOVE the BASS staff.

My name is D. I am just ABOVE C, in the middle of the TWO BLACK KEYS. My note is in the space BELOW the TREBLE staff.

Rhythm Pattern for "New Note Rock"

Count 1 2 1 2 1 2 1 2

Clap hands for each note and count aloud.
Do NOT clap the quarter rest.

New Note Rock

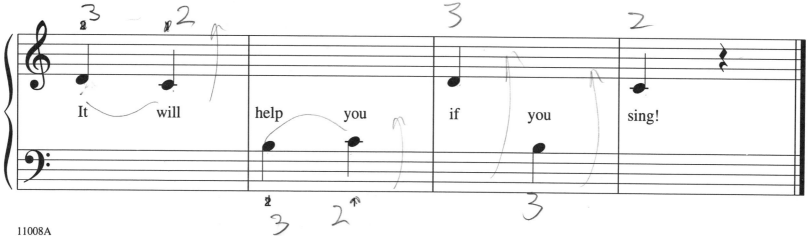

Learn - ing new notes is the thing.

It will help you if you sing!

New Time Signature – $\frac{4}{4}$

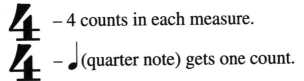

– 4 counts in each measure.

– ♩ (quarter note) gets one count.

– ♪ (quarter rest) also gets one count.

Rhythm Drills in $\frac{4}{4}$

Clap hands for each note and count aloud. Do NOT clap the rests.

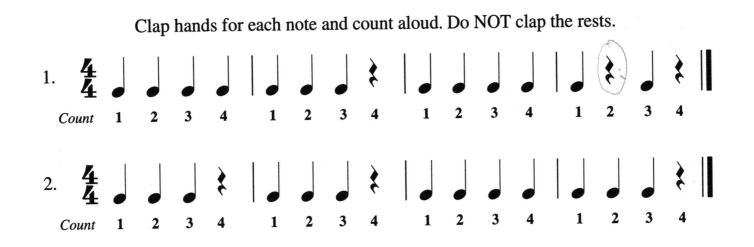

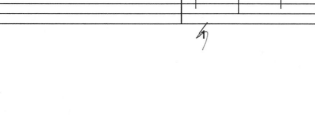

Rhythm Pattern for "Having Fun"

Count 1 2 3 4   1 2 3 4   1 2 3 4   1 2 3 4

Clap hands for each note. Do NOT clap the quarter rest.

Having Fun

New Notes – A and E

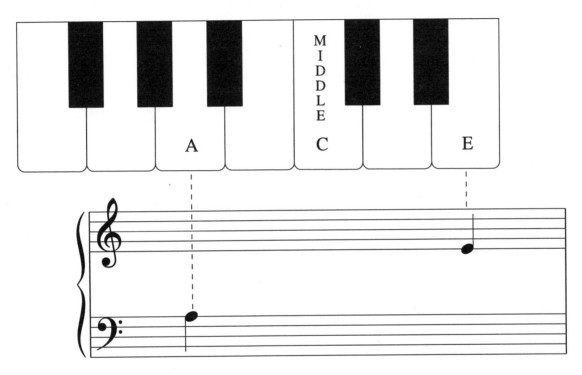

My name is A. I am the white key between the second and third black keys of the THREE BLACK KEYS. My note is on the FIFTH LINE of the BASS staff.

My name is E. I am the white key to the RIGHT of the TWO BLACK KEYS. My note is on the FIRST LINE of the TREBLE staff.

Rhythm Pattern for "Step Right Up"

Count 1 2 3 4   1 2 3 4   1 2 3 4   1 2 3 4

Clap hands for each note and count aloud. Do NOT clap the rests.

Step Right Up
(Right Hand Solo)

Step right up   and you'll see   we can learn notes   eas - i - ly.

Up a - gain,   down and then,   we are real - ly   learn - ing them.

New Note Values

(Remember: ♩ Quarter note = one count)

♩ Half note = two counts

o Whole note = four counts

More Rhythm Drills

Clap hands for each note and count aloud.

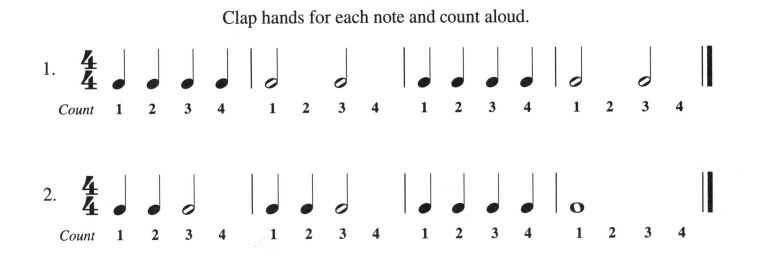

Up and Down

Michelle 9/60   3 times

Rhythm Pattern for "A B C"

Count 1 2 3 4   1 2 3 4   1 2 3 4   1 2 3 4

Clap hands for each note and count aloud.

A B C
(Left Hand Solo)

A   B   C,   Can't you   see,   I   can   say   my   A   B   C.

C   B   A,   C   B   A,   I   can   say   it   eith - er   way.

New Notes – F and G

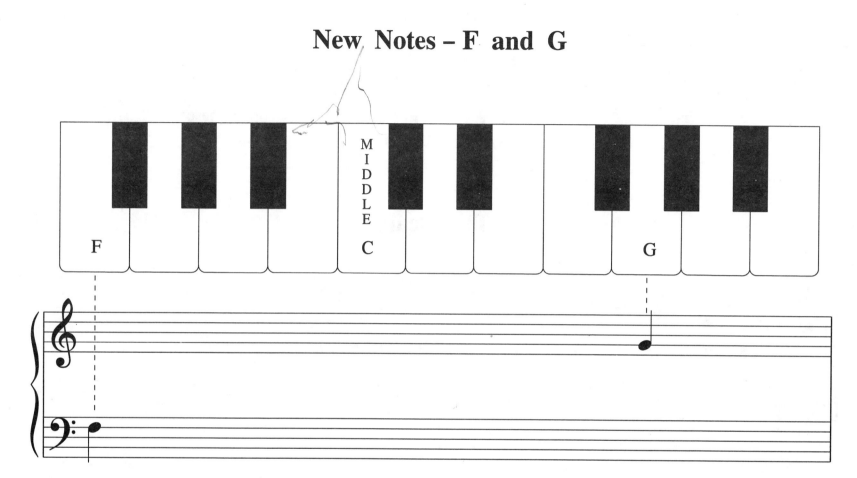

My name is F. I am the white key on the LEFT side of the THREE BLACK KEYS. My note is on the FOURTH LINE of the BASS staff.

My name is G. I am the white key between the first and second black keys of the THREE BLACK KEYS. My note is on the SECOND LINE of the TREBLE staff.

Music Quiz

There is a NEW NOTE in the RIGHT HAND. Is it on a line or space? What is the name of the note? Which line or space is it on?

There is also a NEW NOTE in the LEFT HAND. Is it on a line or space? What is the name of the note? Which line or space is it on?

The Scale

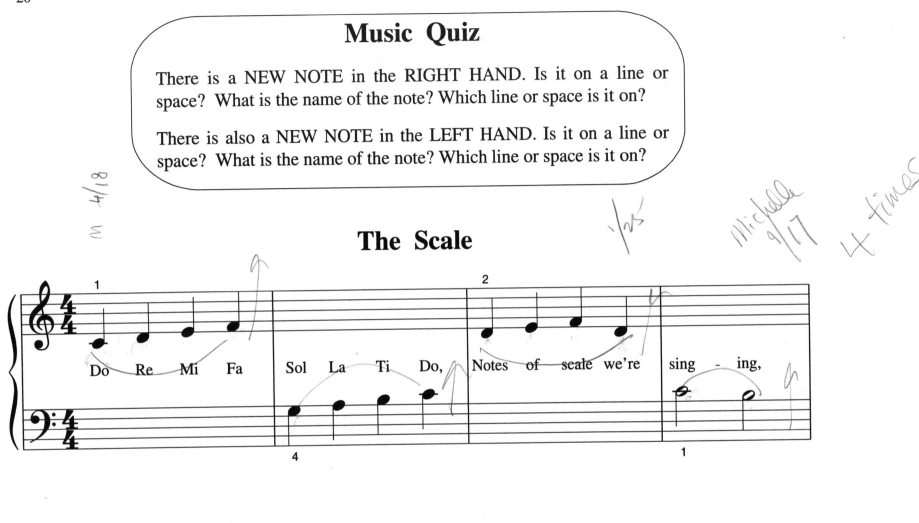

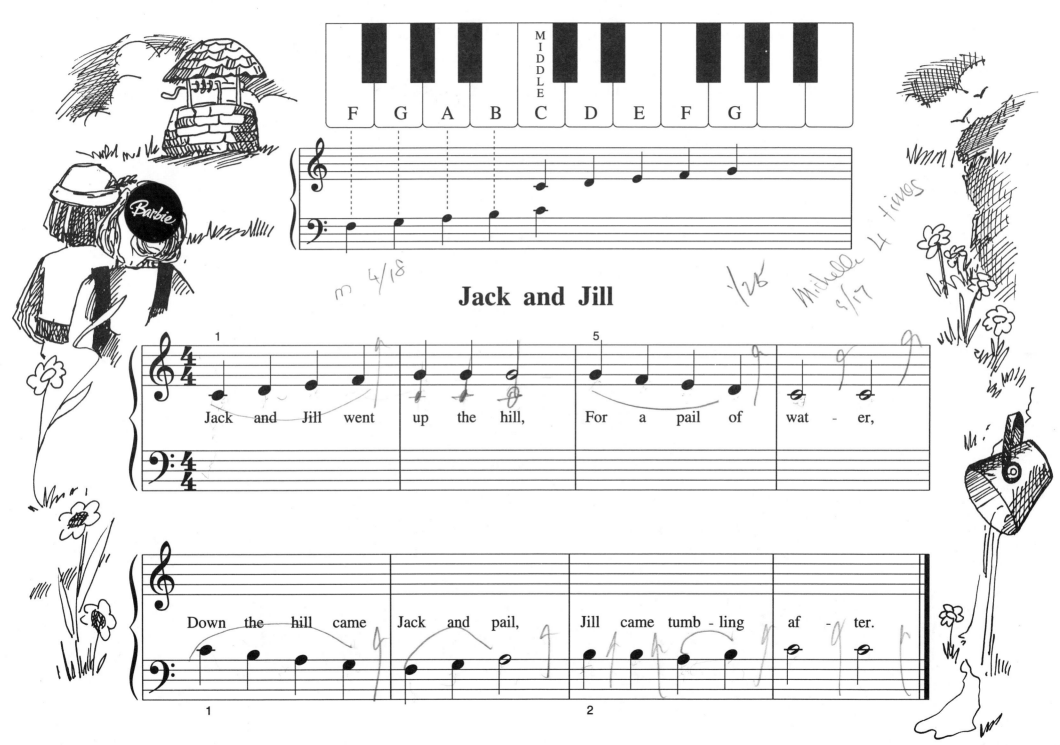

Jack and Jill

New Time Signature – $\frac{3}{4}$

3 – 3 counts in each measure.

4 – ♩ (quarter note) gets one count.

    – 𝄽 (quarter rest) also gets one count.

    – ♩ (half note) gets two counts.

    – ♩. (dotted half note) gets three counts.

Rhythm Drills in $\frac{3}{4}$

Clap hands for each note and count aloud.

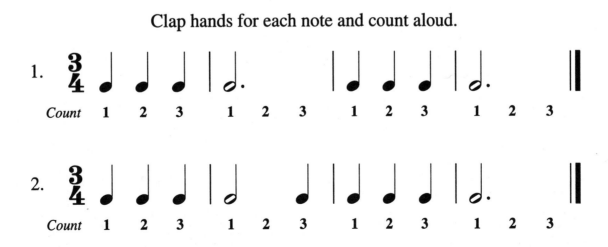

Rhythm Pattern for "Three Kittens"

Clap hands for each note and count aloud.

Three Kittens

Sailing Day

The Baseball Game

Old MacDonald's Farm

Old Mac - Don - ald had a farm, E I E I O, And

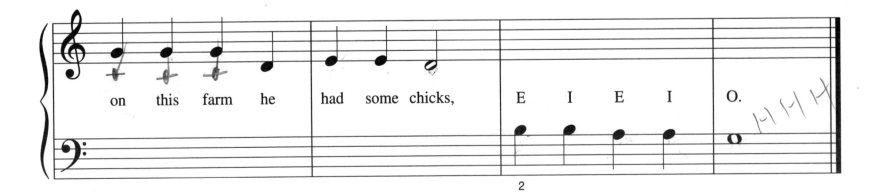

on this farm he had some chicks, E I E I O.

Yankee Doodle

G Position

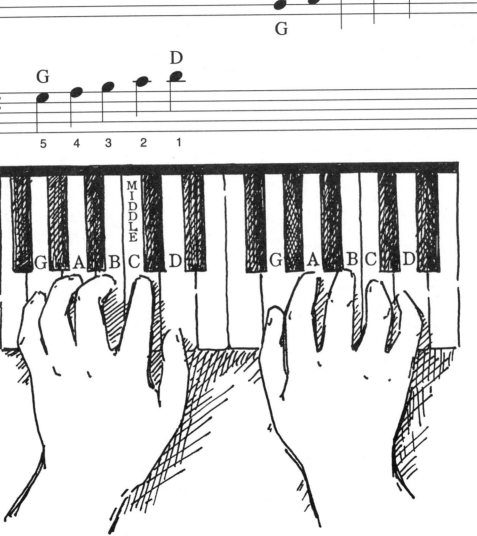

Notice the new way to write D. It is in the space above Middle C.

In this new position, LEFT HAND 5 is on the G below Middle C.
RIGHT HAND 1 is on G above middle C.

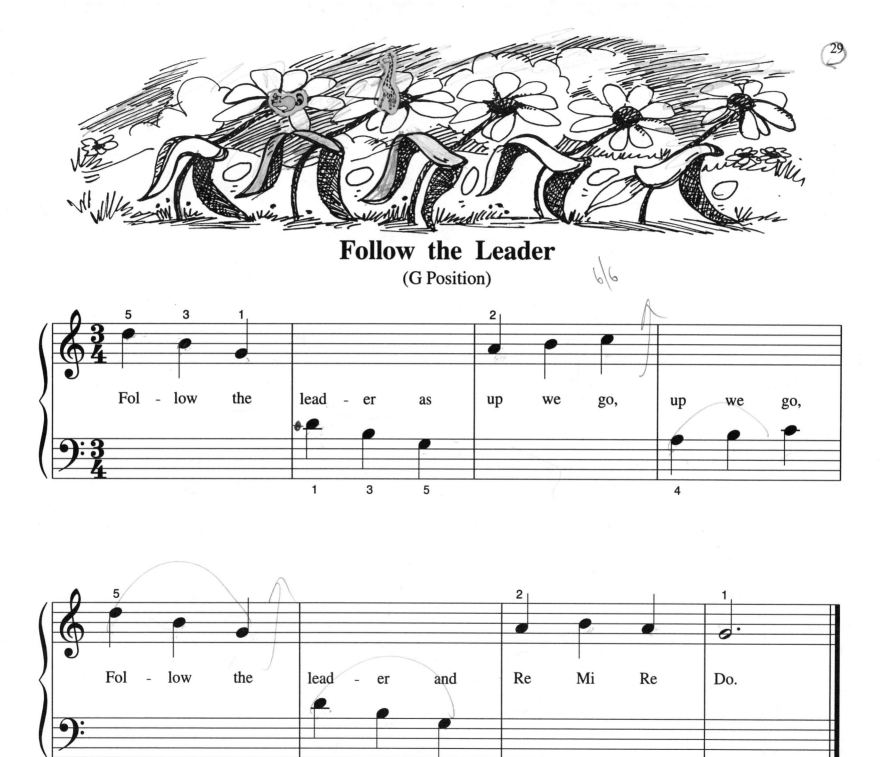

Follow the Leader

(G Position)

Moving Right Along

Tak - ing off and push - ing for - ward, Who knows where I'm go - ing?

Wheel - ing, roll - ing, track - ing, turn - ing, Where the wind is blow - ing.

Song of Sunshine

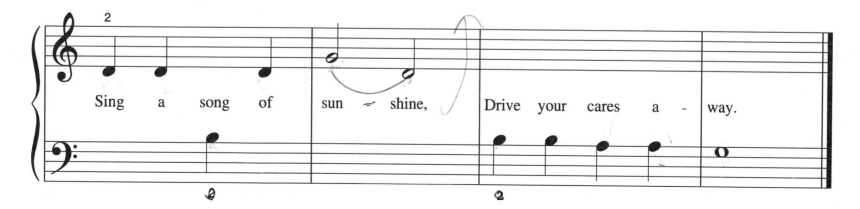

Sing a song of sun - shine, Sing it ev - 'ry day,

Sing a song of sun - shine, Drive your cares a - way.

Lightly Row

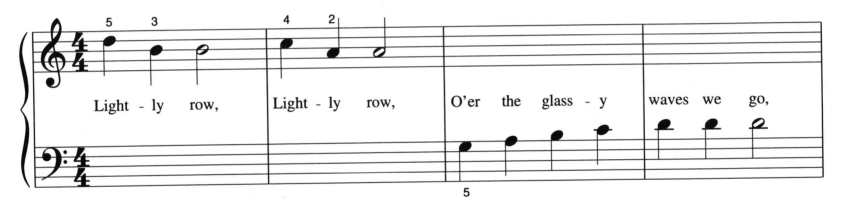

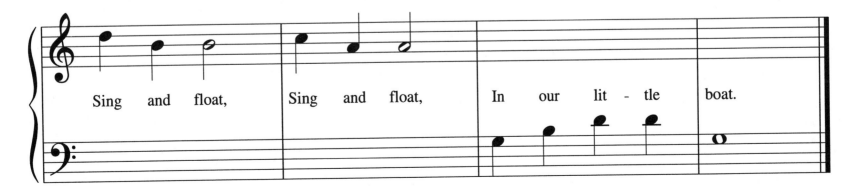

Boy of China

Lit - tle boy of Chi - na, Oh so far a - way,

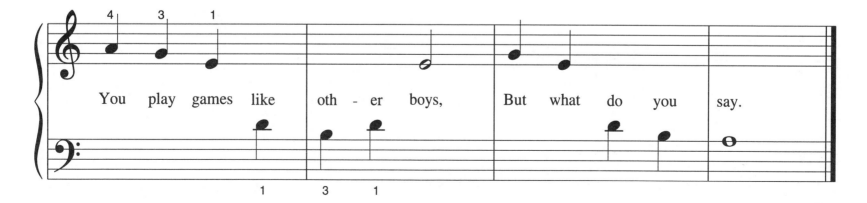

You play games like oth - er boys, But what do you say.

STACCATO, shown by a dot above or below a note, means to release that note quickly.

The Talking Clock

Mary Had a Little Lamb

Mar - y had a lit - tle lamb, Lit - tle lamb, Lit - tle lamb,

Mar - y had a lit - tle lamb, Its fleece was white as snow.

Jolly Old Saint Nicholas

When the clock is strik - ing twelve, When I'm fast a - sleep,

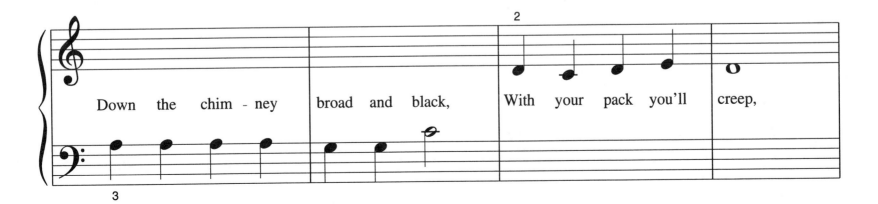

Down the chim - ney broad and black, With your pack you'll creep,

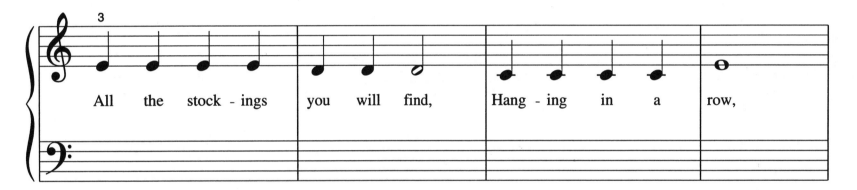

All the stock - ings you will find, Hang - ing in a row,

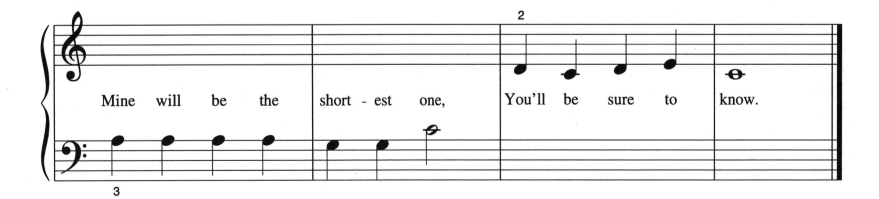

Mine will be the short - est one, You'll be sure to know.

38

Twinkle, Twinkle, Little Star

Notice the stretch and new note.

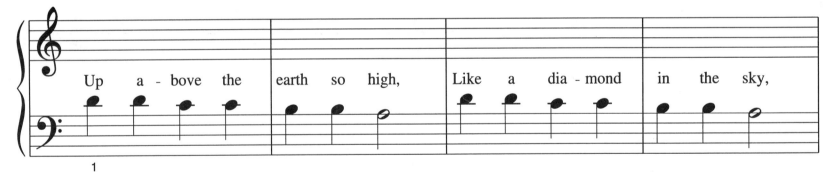

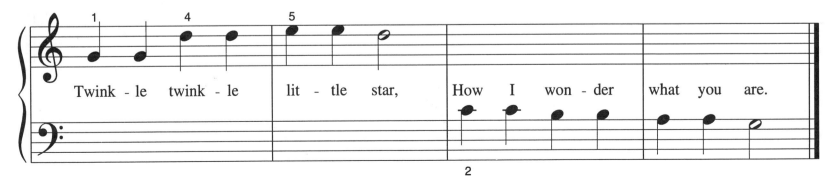

11008A

New C Position

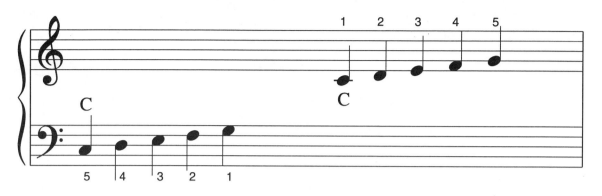

LEFT HAND 5 is on the C below Middle C.

(This is a left hand note, even though the stem goes up.)

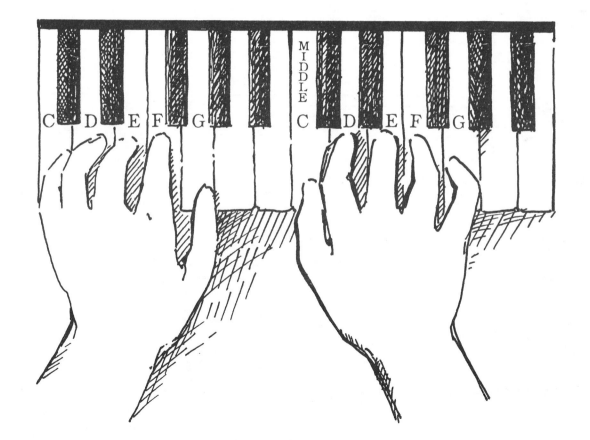

The Banjo

Make your pi - a - no sound just like a ban - jo by

play - ing stac - ca - to. Won't you sing a - long?

Follow the Leader
(C Position)

Now go back to page 29 and play that version of "Follow the Leader."
How are they different? How are they the same?

The Three Cs

3rd Space C

Middle C

2nd Space C

Find and play each C
on your keyboard.

Ding Dong

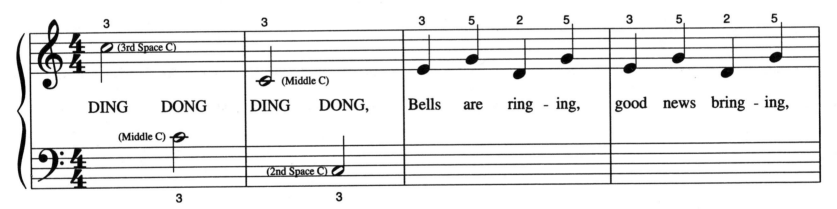

DING DONG   DING DONG,   Bells   are   ring - ing,   good news bring - ing,

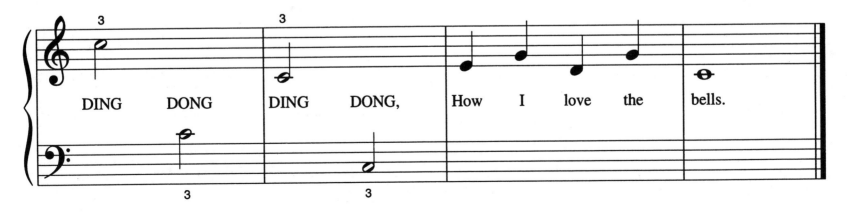

DING   DONG   DING   DONG,   How   I   love   the   bells.

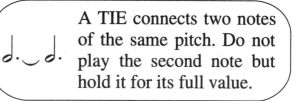

A TIE connects two notes of the same pitch. Do not play the second note but hold it for its full value.

Sleep, Baby, Sleep

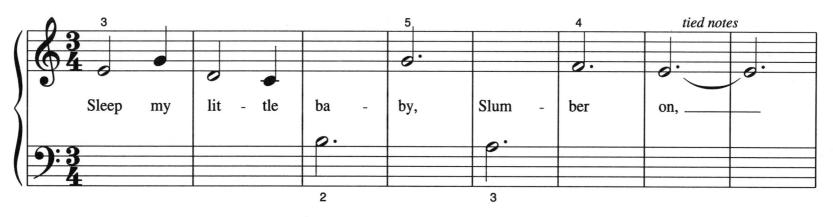

Sleep my lit - tle ba - by, Slum - ber on, _____

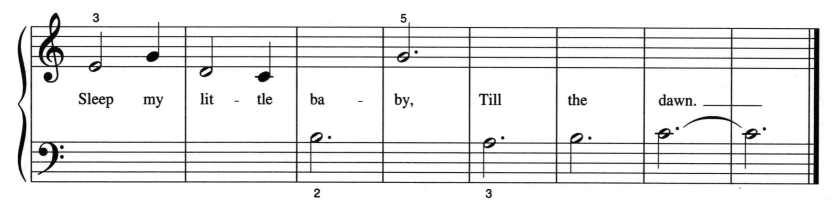

Sleep my lit - tle ba - by, Till the dawn. _____

Practicing

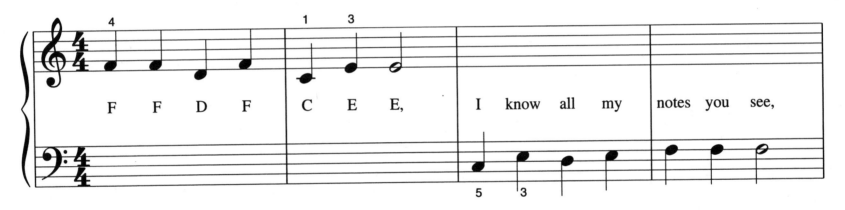

F F D F | C E E, | I know all my | notes you see,

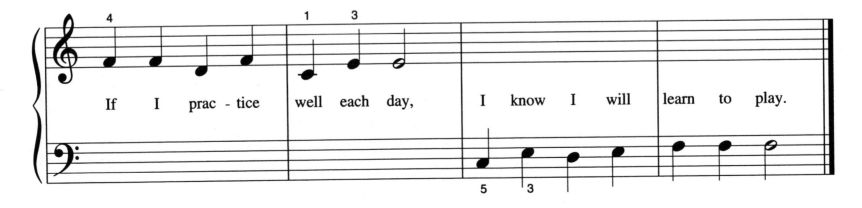

If I prac - tice | well each day, | I know I will | learn to play.

This piece begins on the count of 4. This is called an UPBEAT or a PICK-UP. Notice that the last measure of the piece has only three beats.

Is It Spring?

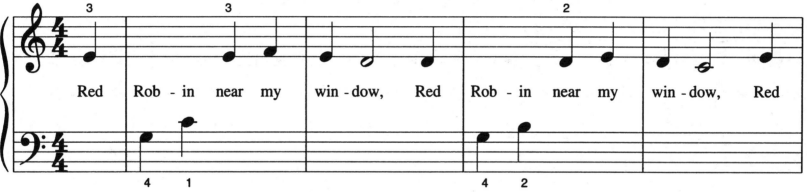

Red Rob - in near my win - dow, Red Rob - in near my win - dow, Red

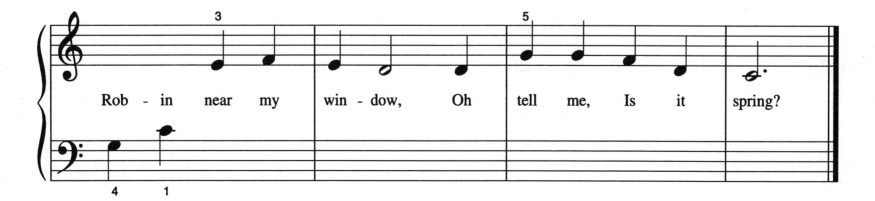

Rob - in near my win - dow, Oh tell me, Is it spring?

The Woodpecker

What is the name of the starting note?

Tap tap tap goes Wood-peck-er, Bus-y all day long, ___

"Wake up now it's time to work," Says your lit-tle song.

Where Is My Doggie?

Certificate
of
Achievement

This certifies that

_____

has successfully completed the Primer Level of

The Michael Aaron Piano Course

and is now ready to begin

Grade One

The
Michael
Aaron
Piano
Course

Teacher _____

Date _____